ON PURPOSE!

UNDERSTANDING YOUR DIVINE DESTINY

ALAN MUSHEGAN, JR.

ON PURPOSE!

ISBN: 0-9755311-5-8

Published by

LIFEBRIDGE
BOOKS
P.O. BOX 49428
CHARLOTTE, NC 28277

Printed in the United States of America.

DEDICATION

To my church family
for their love and support.

Contents

INTRODUCTION

Sooner or later—hopefully sooner— we all come face to face with the basic questions of life:

- Who am I?
- Why was I born?
- What is my purpose on this earth?

The answers are not found in the writings of philosophers, self-help gurus or even personal introspection. As you will discover on these pages, your destiny was planned long before you were born and your Maker is the only One who can reveal your future.

I'm thrilled to share the steps you can take so your growth and development is in lock-step with God's unique plan for your tomorrow.

It makes no difference where you were born, the background of your family, your education or social status. All that matters is that you discover the dream and vision the Almighty has just for you.

God always operates with an ultimate objective in mind—not just for the world, but for you personally.

In these chapters you will find answers to:

- How can I uncover my hidden purpose?
- What are the keys to finding the true meaning of my existence?
- How can I unleash the power of my dream?
- How can I make certain my choices are in step with God's will?
- What specific steps can I take to help me discover my future?

I don't believe you are reading this book by chance. Just as the Lord has inspired me to write these words, I feel He has placed this in your hands—*on purpose!*

Thanks for allowing me to share this time with you.

– Alan Mushegan, Jr.

CHAPTER 1

YOUR DIVINE DESTINY

You are not a mistake! That fact you are alive and breathing on this earth is not the result of a random chance or an accident.

It does not matter where you were birthed, or what your ethnicity, you were created on purpose.

Why am I so certain? It is because everything God does He performs with an ultimate objective in mind. He's the Alpha and the Omega and knows the end from the beginning.

YOU'VE ALWAYS HAD A PURPOSE

From the time I was a small child, I can remember feeling as though my life had special meaning, even a sense of divine destiny. However, it took a while for me to figure it out!

Then one day I read these amazing words in the Bible:

For those God foreknew he also predestined to be conformed to the likeness of his Son, that he might be the firstborn among many brothers.

– Romans 8:29

This means as a child of God, you have *always* had a reason for being.

THE POWER OF A DREAM

One of my favorite characters of the Old Testament is Joseph—the esteemed son of his father, Jacob.

When Joseph was a young boy, his dad showered him with favor. So much so that his brothers became extremely jealous. It is recorded:

When his brothers saw that their father loved him more than any of them, they hated him and could not speak a kind word to him.

– Genesis 37:4

Joseph was a dreamer—and the Lord gave him a clear vision of his future. One of his dreams seemed so outlandish that no one in his family accepted it, not even Jacob. They openly laughed at him and thought he had visions of grandeur, possessing a sense of false pride.

What was this dream? At the age of seventeen, God showed Joseph that one day his brothers would actually bow down before him. (Genesis 37:9).

You can imagine how well that went over!

A short while later, Joseph went out to the fields where his brothers were tending sheep. That's when they plotted to kill him—but instead wound up selling Joseph as a slave to the owner of a caravan headed for Egypt.

When God gives you a dream, there will always be those who try to destroy your vision and stomp out your life's purpose.

GOD MEANT IT FOR GOOD!

I believe this story is included in the Bible because of the important message it contains: When God gives you a dream there will always be those who try to destroy your vision and stomp out your life's purpose. They won't give a second thought to throwing you in a pit!

Keep reading Joseph's incredible life journey and you'll see how much he endured before the day finally dawned when his brothers *did* bow before him—not knowing their thirty-year-old sibling had been appointed by Pharaoh as the governor of Egypt!

Because of his elevated new position, Joseph was able to grant the request of his brothers to purchase enormous amounts of food to take back to the drought-ridden, starving people of Judah. He told them:

> ***You intended to harm me, but God intended it for good to accomplish what is now being done, the saving of many lives.***
> *– Genesis 50:20*

None of this was mere happenstance or coincidence. In God's divine order, everything has a purpose!

FAILURES ARE OPPORTUNITIES

Please don't misunderstand me. God doesn't cause bad things to strike us, or deliberately plan for harm and failure to enter our lives. Even events that may be accompanied by agony and suffering can be turned into something for our good.

Do you remember the story of Job? It wasn't the Lord who punished him. Instead He *allowed* Satan to bring torment so that the faith and trust of this godly servant could be demonstrated.

Through it all, Job was able to say:

Though he slay me, yet will I trust in him.
–Job 13:15 KJV

In God's infinite wisdom, He can take our difficult circumstances and turn them into our benefit—and His.

In God's infinite wisdom, He can take our difficult circumstances and turn them into our benefit —and His.

The key is: we must continue to follow His plan, never our own. The only *true* failures of life are those who neglect to see the hand of God at work and continue to wallow in the aftermath of their mistakes. The Lord knows we might fall off the rails, so He has made provision to help us get back on track.

My earthly father has drilled this into my consciousness since I was a child: "Don't allow your failures to stop you; rather use them as stepping stones to greatness."

With the right perspective, every error or mistake will give us a deeper sense of purpose—an opportunity to learn and grow. Why? Because in God's eyes we are *never* failures.

The apostle Paul was shipwrecked, beaten and persecuted for the cause of Christ, yet was still able to declare:

> ***And we know that all things work together for good to them that love God, to them who are the called according to his purpose.***
>
> *– Romans 8:28 KJV*

You can unlock the door to success by identifying what you have been doing *wrong* and making a vow to start, with God's guidance, on a path toward true excellence.

Regardless of your lot in life, see yourself on a road leading to a worthy destination. When things go wrong, remember that you're not *in* trouble, you're just passing *through.* What did David say when his world began to crumble?

Even though I walk through the valley of the shadow of death, I will fear no evil, for you are with me; your rod and your staff, they comfort me.
– Psalm 23:4

The next time your nose hits a brick wall, give yourself a pep talk. "This will ultimately help me. With God by my side, I'm going *through* it!"

AGAINST THE ROPES

More than once I've watched a heavyweight boxing match on television and witnessed a fighter literally leaning on the ropes exhausted—ready for those in his corner to throw in the towel.

In truth, it is on those ropes a champion finds out what *stuff* he is made of. To some, it is a sign of defeat, to others it propels them to victory.

Mohamed Ali used the ropes as a clever strategy.

He would lean against them to lure his opponent into a false complacency—then, out of nowhere, Ali would deliver a powerful knockout blow. They even coined a phrase after his slick deception; it's called "rope-a-dope."

This all-time greatest fighter who could "float like a butterfly and sting like a bee," had practiced so much against the ropes he did not see it as a negative.

Some give up on the sidelines of life while others bounce back with surprising agility. What about you? If you feel you are dangling precariously on life's ropes, start using them to your advantage. They can help you bounce back and triumph!

BORN TO LOSE?

I once saw a man with a tattoo on his arm that read "Born to Lose."

To me it was a tragic waste of ink—even a self-fulfilling prophecy! If only this man could realize the Almighty never creates someone for failure. We were born to succeed, to win, to triumph and take our rightful place as God's children.

The Bible declares:

> ***...we are more than conquerors through him who loved us.***
>
> *– Romans 8:37*

How sad to come to the conclusion, "I'm stuck in a rut of failure and can never escape!"

Don't believe that lie. It's not true. Since God is "not a respecter of persons" we all have the same opportunities on the earth He created. The Lord doesn't go around with a rubber stamp in His hand and label one person "Loser" and another "Winner." We are all equally precious in His sight.

The Lord doesn't go around with a rubber stamp in His hand and label one person "Loser" and another "Winner."

It's not necessary to be born with a silver spoon in your mouth in order to rise to the top. Start reading the biographies of great men and women and you'll find most were born into average families and succeeded through a combination of faith, perseverance and an undying determination to achieve their God-given potential. It's true in sports, education, business, government and virtually every category of achievement.

You may think some made it on "a wing and a prayer," but I say they made it *on purpose*.

WHAT'S DRIVING YOU?

The only way you'll ever reach your dream is to be totally driven by a passion and desire.

James, the brother of Jesus, counsels that we shouldn't be moved by every wind that blows our direction (James 1:6)—and certainly not by our own desires, nor by the things we see or experience.

If you plan to walk in your divine purpose, your motivation must come from within and be birthed by the Spirit of God.

After Jesus explained salvation to Nicodemus, He told him it resembles a *"wind"* (John 3:8), but when the promised Holy Spirit descended, here is how witnesses described the scene in the Upper Room:

> ***And suddenly there came a sound from heaven as of a rushing mighty wind, and it filled all the house where they were sitting.***
>
> *– Acts 2:2 KJV*

It wasn't just a breeze, rather a wind that was powerful and active!

Life's sea isn't always tranquil. Make sure what floats your boat is not a *world*-driven gust, but a cloud by day and a fire by night which comes directly from God Himself.

POSITIONED FOR GREATNESS

While you are living on this earth, your calendar is dictated by a schedule the Almighty put together at creation. He declares:

There is a time for everything, and a season for every activity under heaven.
– Ecclesiastes 3:1

Regardless of the *season* you are in at this moment, understand if you are in Christ, you are being positioned for greatness.

Even in times of sorrow and uncertainty, don't panic. You're right where you need to be in the Lord's "DayTimer."

To our finite brains this can be rather confusing. But we must, by faith, believe the Word of God when it tells us if the Lord is mindful of the birds of the air and the lilies of the field, He also knows what we are going through.

Friend, the same God who is with you on the mountain top is walking beside you in your most pressing hour of need.

Think about David who, after being anointed as the next king of Israel, spent a long time hiding from King Saul who was plotting to assassinate him. For about nine years David made his home in dens and caves, yet all the time God was positioning him for greatness.

UNDERSTANDING THE TIME

We have all heard the stories of those who were "in the right place at the right time."

It's all about timing —not yours, God's.

This is especially true for fulfilling the purpose and plan for your future. It's all about timing—not yours, *God's!*

Esther is a perfect example.

In the Old Testament account, she was a young virgin selected from her province to be taken to the house of the ungodly King Xeres. As fate would have it, the king had appointed officers in all the territories of his kingdom to handpick the finest maidens in the land so he could find himself a new queen.

After a rigorous purification process Esther was presented to the king and he favored her above all the other women in his palace. She was a Jewish girl, something the ruler wasn't aware of. Esther didn't know it at the time, but her entire purpose for being in the kings house was to save her people from total annihilation.

Eventually, understanding the enormity of the situation and listening to her uncle Mordecai, she was able to fulfill her calling.

The most important passage in the story of Esther is the advice she received from Mordecai when he said:

> ***And who knows but that you have come to*** [a] ***royal position for such a time as this?***
> *– Esther 4:14*

When the light of this truth dawned on Esther, she finally understood her destiny. God had placed her in the *right place* at the *right time* to be selected as queen so she could spare her people and uncover the plot of Haman.

All she endured—being taken from her family, suffering through the purification process and finding the favor of the king—brought her to a point where she had new insight, recognizing God's timing for her life. Because of this, Haman was hung on his own gallows and her people were set free.

Never take for granted the season you are currently passing through. It's far more important to ask, "What's on God's calendar for me?"

Chapter 2

Get the Picture?

I don't know about you but I love watching movies. Let me go ahead and confess—sometimes I watch three or four movies a week. I must be Blockbuster's favorite customer!

For me, it's a way to unwind and relax my mind. For a few hours it is an escape—getting involved in the life of someone else and not being forced to think about my own.

One thing I've noticed about every movie I have seen is that each film has a beginning and an end — and there are several plot-points which help develop the drama so the viewer can sense the direction of the movie; to see where the story is going. All these factors combine to create the "big picture."

However, in the final analysis, what separates a "dud" from an Oscar nominee is the vision of the director. You can have a great screenplay based on a bestselling novel, produced by a stellar company, but if the director cannot capture the vision for the movie-goer, it will be a flop.

IT'S YOUR STORY

Much like a movie there is a big picture for your life. Just as a film, there are opening and closing credits, but somewhere in the middle you have to choose how you are going to develop the plot—scene after scene—so you can reach your expected conclusion.

In our personal movie the Holy Spirit is the Director, Jesus is the Writer, and God is the Producer.

Here's the bottom line: if you don't have vision for your future you are going to fail, no matter how good the screenplay.

In our personal movie the Holy Spirit is the Director, Jesus is the Writer, and God is the Producer. The vision is firmly in place. Now it is up to you to see the plot-points so you will be able to better understand your true purpose. How it all plays out is up to the choices you make along the way and your ability to understand what has been written and what is in the heart and soul of the producer.

Get the picture?

What is Vision?

Have you ever watched a 3-D movie in a theater? When you are wearing those funny glasses with two-colored lens, objects on the screen seem to spring to life—as if they are protruding from the screen.

What used to be two-dimensional is now popping out at you. However, when you remove the glasses, the screen is a distorted mess. The images appear out of focus and there are extra colored lines which make the picture fuzzy.

The same is true of life. There are events that often become blurry, and squiggly lines are layered over the already confused pictures of who we are and where we're headed.

Thank God, there is an answer. When we put on the supernatural glasses of the Holy Spirit, that which was unclear and indistinct, now becomes so real we can reach out and touch it. What once was hidden is now revealed—we begin to see in a new dimension!

But as it is written, Eye hath not seen, nor ear heard, neither have entered into the heart of man, the things which God hath prepared for them that love Him. But God hath revealed them unto us by His Spirit [our 3-D glasses]*: for the Spirit searcheth all things, yea, the deep things of God.*

– 1 Corinthians 2:9-10 KJV

There are certain things God has planned for us only *He* can reveal. We will never be able to see them without His supernatural help.

This leads us to the true meaning of vision—the revelation (or revealing) of what we cannot see with our natural mind or our physical eyes. There are three dimensions involved.

LOOK TO THE SOURCE

First, the most important point we need to understand about vision is that it comes from God. It can't be self-produced.

One evening while I was relaxing watching one of my favorite television shows, my cable went out and suddenly everything on the screen was scrambled. What did I do? Well, I sat there trying to imagine what was happening on the program.

Even though I have a vivid imagination, I was frustrated because no matter how hard I tried, I couldn't see the picture.

As we grow and develop, we can't just guess what we are supposed to do, we need to *see* it. This is where God comes in.

The Lord...wants to give you a revelation—a sneak peak—of what lies ahead.

Vision is not something you concoct or make up; instead, it is a reality that already exists in the mind of your Creator—a picture only He can give you.

Think of it! The Lord has planned your future from the beginning of time and He wants to give you a revelation—a sneak-peak—of what lies ahead.

IT'S ESSENTIAL!

The second fact you need to know concerning

spiritual vision is that you cannot live productively and reach your destiny without it. The Bible says:

> ***Where there is no vision, the people perish...***
> *– Proverbs 29:18 KJV*

In Hebrew the word for *perish* is *para,* meaning naked. Vision literally clothes us with purpose and the anointing of the Spirit we need to reach and fulfill our God-ordained potential.

THE FAITH FACTOR

Third, we need to comprehend that vision is an element of faith. Here's the biblical definition:

> ***Now faith is the substance of things hoped for, the evidence of things not seen.***
> *– Hebrews 11:1 KJV*

It's the revealing of things not seen which is the *evidence* of faith. Vision is a "spirit eye" allowing us to see with God's 3-D glasses.

Again, the three dimensions are:

1. Vision comes from God.
2. Vision is necessary for a productive life.
3. Vision is part of faith.

INSTANT REPLAY

What a miracle of technology. We can click a few buttons and play back all the programs or films we love to watch. Even if we're interrupted by an urgent phone call it doesn't matter. We just hit the record button and catch the action later without skipping a beat!

Here's what I've noticed when watching a movie more than once—every time I see it again I pick up on something new, wondering, "How did I miss that?"

If you want to find a coach on the weekend after a big football game, look in the film room. There he is, intently watching each play in slow motion, frame by frame, trying to catch every mistake so he can prepare his players for next week's contest.

Even as a spectator, whether it's football, baseball, basketball or hockey, we wait for the instant replays to get a closer look at the action.

It is important to *review* your vision—again and

again—so you will be able to see all the angles and moves you need to make to achieve the ultimate goal.

MID-COURSE CORRECTIONS

On the many film lots of Hollywood, during the production of movies, the directors watch something called "dalies."

These are rush prints of the last few hours' work so they can examine their daily progress—and make mid-course corrections. It's the only way to know if they're getting it right and are faithfully executing what was originally envisioned.

Are you replaying the divine script written for you? Are you constantly making sure you're doing everything possible to reach your objective for *today?* This is important because the more you look at your vision the greater the revelation.

Go ahead! Roll it over and over in your mind—evaluating every step you have taken to date. In the process I guarantee you'll see more of what you should be doing to make God's dream a reality.

The Bible tells us to:

Write the vision, and make it plain upon tables, that he may run that readeth it.

– Habakkuk 2:2 KJV

God's plan for you must become *tangible* so you won't forget what you have seen through the eyes of faith. That's how we move forward—even *running* with the vision.

FILL IN THE BLANKS

Let me emphasize that only when you see the whole story will you be able to recognize the plot points—or what I like to call "moments of destiny." Most people exist one day at a time and fail to recognize the critical turning-point junctures. They seem totally unaware of the larger scope of things.

God's plan for you must become tangible so you won't forget what you have seen through the eyes of faith.

Have you ever played "Fill in the blanks"? In this game you are given only part of a quote or a phrase and you have to come up with what is missing.

There are several popular versions of this

activity—Wheel of Fortune, hangman, even crossword puzzles.

Let me share this secret. Your life and vision is much like playing one of these games, but on a much grander scale. The apostle Paul writes:

> ***For we know in part and we prophesy in part, but when perfection comes, the imperfect disappears. When I was a child, I talked like a child, I thought like a child, I reasoned like a child. When I became a man, I put childish ways behind me. Now we see but a poor reflection as in a mirror; then we shall see face to face. Now I know in part; then I shall know fully, even as I am fully known.***
>
> *– 1 Corinthians 13:9-12*

A SUPERNATURAL REVELATION

During our trek on this earth we only see a small part of the overall panorama—and the rest remains obscured. One day, however, the curtains will be drawn back and the entire picture will be visible.

Until that time we are to "fill in the blanks" as they are revealed by God's Spirit.

This is where being constantly sensitive to the things of the Lord is essential. It's not what you *can* see that requires heavenly insight, but what you *can't!*

For that which is still a mystery, go ahead and say, "Okay Lord, fill in the blanks!"

For that which is still a mystery, go ahead and say, "Okay Lord, fill in the blanks!"

The missing pieces of our destiny will *remain* that way until they are supernaturally revealed. How does this happen? The Spirit of the Lord unveils them by giving us *"the spirit of wisdom and revelation in the knowledge of him"* (Ephesians. 1:17).

Earnestly pray, asking the Lord to allow you to move into these three key areas of the Spirit:

1. Wisdom.
2. Knowledge.
3. Revelation.

This will bring you to a brand new level of understanding—and permit you to see what has been missing from your life.

DO WE REALLY UNDERSTAND?

When you walk into the entrance of a mega-mall there's usually a store directory right inside the door equipped with map and an arrow pointing: "You Are Here."

Why is the arrow important? Because if you don't have a clue where you *are,* how will you ever know how to reach your destination?

With the parts of the puzzle supplied by God —wisdom, knowledge and revelation—you will have a comprehension of your present location and be oriented to finding the direction that leads to your ultimate purpose.

This is vital since you can only move forward at the level of your understanding.

Long ago, King Solomon wrote:

My son, if you accept my words and store up my commands within you, turning your ear to wisdom and applying your heart to understanding, and if you call out for insight and cry aloud for understanding, and if you look for it as for silver and search for it as for hidden treasure, then

you will understand the fear of the Lord and find the knowledge of God. For the Lord gives wisdom, and from his mouth come knowledge and understanding.

– Proverbs 2:1-6

IS IT CHILDISH?

You would never take a child, strap him in behind the wheel of a new Buick and say "Drive!"

Of course, not. Apart from the fact it is against the law, the youngster has neither the knowledge nor the skill to navigate on the road—no matter how clearly it is marked or how smooth it is paved.

Likewise, you wouldn't take a junior high student to the boardroom of a major corporation and announce, "We're putting you in charge. Run the company!"

Why? Because a child moves like a child, responds as a child, and has the comprehension of a child.

But when we push the calendar forward a few years, that same boy or girl is now driving the car and running the company. What makes the difference? Is it their age? No, something far more is involved —*maturity* and *understanding.*

The apostle Paul prayed:

...that the body of Christ may be built up until we all reach unity in the faith and in the knowledge of the Son of God and become mature, attaining to the whole measure of the fullness of Christ.
– Ephesians 4:12-13

As sons and daughters of God we can only operate at the level of understanding He has given us. So what do we need? It's the Lord's desire:

...that the eyes of your heart may be enlightened in order that you may know the hope to which he has called you, the riches of his glorious inheritance in the saints.
– Ephesians 1:18

THE MASTER NAVIGATOR!

When God expands our spiritual sight by increasing our understanding we begin to realize what we are capable of accomplishing. As we *see* more we will *achieve* more.

The words "ask" "seek" and "receive" are essential in knowing God's perfect will and plan. In addition, we need to keep the door of our heart wide open—

an invitation for the Lord to pour in whatever He desires.

To me, receiving guidance from the Lord is like riding in a car with someone giving you directions as you drive. If you pay attention and listen carefully you'll know exactly where to turn and the route to follow. As a result, you'll reach a destination you could never find on your own.

I'm glad the "Master Navigator" is showing me the way!

On the back of a truck I saw this bumper sticker: "God is my Co-Pilot."

I'm glad the "Master Navigator" is showing me the way!

WOULD SOMEBODY PLEASE TURN ON THE LIGHTS!

More than once I've stubbed my toe trying to make it through my bedroom in the pitch of night. Ouch! It can really hurt!

At times, walking through life can produce the same results as we blindly stumble along.

The reason it's no fun to be without light is because

darkness is the enemy of sight. Walking in blackness can leave you confused, depressed, feeling alone and, worst of all, *without vision.*

Think about this. I could place you in a dark room full of priceless treasures, but without your ability to see, you'd never know what is around you or have the chance to enjoy their beauty.

Without Christ we live in an existence of perpetual darkness. It will keep your gift and purpose hidden, even when it is within your grasp. The Word tells us:

> ***But everything exposed by the light becomes visible, for it is light that makes everything visible. This is why it is said: "Wake up, O sleeper, rise from the dead, and Christ will shine on you."***
>
> *– Ephesians 5:13-14*

A productive existence begins by flipping on the switch! When God declared, "Let there be light," the world was transformed. And today, it still affects us in positive ways:

- Sunlight causes growth and brings warmth to the earth.

- A light at nighttime takes away fear from an anxious child and helps him to sleep.
- The beacon of light from a lighthouse guides ships safely to port.

If these are the natural benefits, just think what the eternal light of God can do for you!

LIGHT THE LAMP!

What is the source of spiritual sight? And how can we turn on wisdom, knowledge and revelation to see our heaven-determined destiny? The answer is found in scripture. The psalmist writes:

Thy word is a lamp unto my feet, and a light unto my path.
– Psalm 199:105

How comforting to have the road illuminated when I can't see where I'm going. How reassuring to know there is a beacon which brings me the warmth of peace and joy, and causes me to grow.

The Word is the light of God showing us the way which has been prepared. And here's something amazing: the more of God's Word you have within you, the more "brightness" you will possess and reflect. No longer will you be alone, fumbling in the darkness.

- Read the Word.
- Hear the Word.
- Meditate on the Word.

What's inside will shine outward with such a glow and intensity, you will never be lost again. You'll see the picture!

CHAPTER 3

THERE'S A PLAN!

I was teaching a class of teenagers in an upstairs room of the church on a Sunday evening when suddenly someone burst into the back door of the room. "Pastor Alan, Pastor Alan! You are needed in the sanctuary."

"What's the problem? I wanted to know.

"The Bishop says you have the word of the Lord for the church tonight."

As I walked out onto the stage of an arena style building filled with thousands, I began to speak. Instantly, these seven words came out of my mouth—"God has a plan for your life!"

At that moment the Holy Spirit fell across the congregation and they stood to their feet, celebrating the words the Lord had inspired me to speak.

Then, as I continued, the only words I could utter were: "God has a plan for your life!"

At that moment I awoke and realized I had been dreaming. There, in the stillness of my room, I was brought back to reality. I began saying to myself,"I am here for a reason. I am not here by chance, but by design."

"I am here for a reason. I am not here by chance, but by design."

Some people would call this an epiphany—and I believe they are right.

The Lord had truly placed a message in my heart and on my lips. It was a word people needed to hear.

This may seem unusual to some, yet for me it was a definite moment of truth. God was reminding me once again my life had meaning and I had been placed here on earth for a divine purpose.

The instant I awakened there was a whole new perspective on my future. I realized the Lord was imparting *destiny* to me.

WHEN GOD SPEAKS, LISTEN!

If you'll think back, perhaps you can recall the times and places you were given a glimpse of your life's calling—the reason you are here.

I had experienced similar moments earlier. For example, when I was a child I imagined myself performing musically. Then, at the age of fifteen I received a clear, definite call to the ministry.

My eighteenth birthday was truly a red-letter day. I was sitting in church on a Sunday morning when the Lord spoke to me in a way I had never before known. In a vision, He showed me His Church fragmented and torn—saying, "Put My body back together again!"

If your heart is open to hear His voice, God longs to reveal His calling to you.

Moments like these have defined purpose in my life. If your heart is open to hear His voice, God longs to reveal His calling to you.

In the Old Testament, the Lord selected an entire nation—Israel—to be designated as "God's chosen people." Today, individual believers are called by the Father. Peter was speaking directly to us as he writes:

But you are a chosen people, a royal priesthood, a holy nation, a people belonging to God, that you

may declare the praises of him who called you out of darkness into his wonderful light.

– 1 Peter 2:9

MEMORIZE THE MOMENT

Many are so caught up in the present they can't see their future. One of the reasons is they never take the time to recall God's voice at significant junctures in their life.

It's important to know what God is saying today, yet we must never relinquish what He has revealed in the past.

Let me encourage you to keep a "spiritual scrapbook" of the pictures the Lord has painted in your mind. In times of confusion and indecision it will be these mental images that will bring you through critical moments—once more shedding light on your tomorrow.

NEVER FORGET YOUR CALLING

It's important to know what God is saying today, yet we must never relinquish what He has revealed in the past. Without following this principle we will become like those who are so caught up in their daily circumstances they forget the Creator has a total strategy for their life—from birth to eternity!

Many have desires for their future and goals they would like to reach, yet they'll never arrive at God's intended destination because they have forgotten the times they have come face to face with the Lord's calling and direction for their lives.

THE "AMERICAN DREAM"?

Keep coming back to the fact there is something specific you were placed on this earth to accomplish—and it's the only thing which has true value.

There is something specific you were placed on this earth to accomplish—and it's the only thing that has true value.

Our source of power for today and our hope for tomorrow is that God intends for us to be living daily on His unique schedule—the measure of real achievement.

There is much more to life than what many call "The American Dream"— a house with a white picket fence, two kids playing in the yard, growing old with dignity, and accumulating as much wealth as you possibly can.

Don't get me wrong. While all of the above has worth, absolutely nothing can compare with achieving the dream God has uniquely designed just for YOU!

THE MAN WHO HAD EVERYTHING, AND YET HAD NOTHING

One day I sat talking with a gentleman who personally owned more cars, properties, businesses than you can count. He and his family lived in an opulent mansion. Yet, as we continued to talk, I perceived this multi-millionaire was one of the most unfulfilled, dejected individuals I had ever met.

While collecting his "toys," he had never sought God's desire for his life.

Something was desperately missing.

Despite all the accumulation of wealth, success and acclaim, what had this man failed to find? While collecting his "toys," he had never sought God's desire for his life.

He could purchase anything money could buy, yet had never discovered the one treasure which was truly priceless—more valuable than anything he owned.

How tragic he didn't know God had a plan and purpose for his existence.

How tragic he didn't know God had a plan and purpose for his existence.

After meeting him I thought, "What price tag can you place on being fulfilled?

His list of assets were sadly lacking in what really mattered— love, joy, hope and faith. I remembered the words of Jesus:

For what shall it profit a man, if he shall gain the whole world, and lose his own soul?

– Mark 8:36 KJV

FIGHT THE GOOD FIGHT!

We are each created with three distinct parts: spirit, soul and body.

The soul of a man is who he is—his personality and everything inherent within him. So if you amass all the world's wealth yet never find the purpose for which you were born, you're left bankrupt!

What a contrast we see in the life of Paul the apostle.

He was shipwrecked three times, stoned and left for dead, beaten with a whip, bitten by a deadly serpent on the isle of Malta, yet he could not die until the time appointed by God.

Languishing in a prison dungeon, chained like a common criminal and knowing his work was nearly completed, he was able to write these words to Timothy, a son in the Lord:

...the time has come for my departure. I have fought the good fight, I have finished the race, I have kept the faith.

– 2 Timothy 4:6-7

He had found his reason for being—and could die happy because he had carried out his life's mission.

In this final lesson, Paul was saying, "My life is complete because I have accomplished all I have been asked to do."

How could this follower of Christ be so positive, so content? He had found his reason for being—and could die happy because he had carried out his life's mission.

THE PERFECT BLUEPRINT

I once heard a woman say, "I'm not sure I want what God has planned for me."

What a mistaken viewpoint!

She needed to realize that all our man-made choices have perimeters and boundaries. With the Lord, however, you begin an upward journey where not even the sky is the limit—since He rules the heavens and we are His heirs.

What a relief to come to the conclusion the Lord's blueprint is far better than any we could design for ourselves.

What a relief to come to the conclusion the Lord's blueprint is far better than any we could design for ourselves. After all, His way is perfect!

It is God's plan:

- For you to be healthy and physically strong.
- For you to have the right relationships.
- For your family to be tightly knit together.
- For you to prosper.

- For you to be a leader in your home and community.

Most important, it is your Father's greatest desire for you to have a personal relationship with Him. We could not ask for more!

As for God, his way is perfect; the word of the Lord is flawless. He is a shield for all who take refuge in him.

– Psalm 18:30

YOU WERE GOD'S PLAN FROM THE BEGINNING

Of one thing you can be certain: the Father knew you before you were ever born. Remember what God said to the prophet Jeremiah:

Before I formed you in the womb I knew you, before you were born I set you apart; I appointed you as a prophet to the nations.

– Jeremiah 1:5

You have *always* been foremost in His mind. He

not only knew about you, but mapped out a plan for your future. And God doesn't make mistakes.

Just as the sky, ocean, trees and animals have a special reason for being, your life carries an ultimate purpose.

THE IDENTITY CRISIS

A young woman once told me, "I have always struggled with my identity and self-acceptance because my mother told me I was an accident."

"I have always struggled with my identity and self-acceptance because my mother told me I was an accident."

Her mom frequently reminded her how her older brother and sister were the result of planned pregnancies, while she was a complete surprise. As a result, this young lady felt her existence did not carry with it any real meaning.

I reassured her, "You have always been part of what God designed, whether your parents wanted you or not." And I added, "Never forget, your Heavenly Father's plan supersedes whatever decisions your mom and dad did or didn't make."

As I've heard my father say countless times: "There are no failures with God."

Whether your parents lovingly prepared for your arrival or you were a big surprise—whether you were raised in an orphanage or in a happy, two-parent family—the Lord always knew *who you were* and *what you were to become.*

The world was formed with you in mind and you are special to the Creator:

> ***...everyone who is called by my name, whom I created for my glory, whom I formed and made.***
>
> *– Isaiah 43:7*

THE FIRST STEP

"How do I go about finding God's purpose for my life?"

The next logical question is, "How do I go about finding God's purpose for my life?"

It begins by admitting you are a sinner and believing on God's Son for your salvation. It's impossible to walk in His plan without first accepting Christ.

If you do not know Jesus as your Savior and Lord, I invite you to pray this prayer with me—and believe it from your heart:

> *Jesus, I believe You are the Christ the Son of God, that You gave Your life for me and for this world by shedding Your blood on the cross.*
>
> *I believe God raised You, Jesus, from the dead, and that You are alive and are now seated in heavenly places. I thank You for forgiving me of all of my sin. I accept Your will and Your plan for my life.*
>
> *Live in me Lord Jesus. Teach me Your ways. I ask You to be my Lord and Savior and declare I will follow Your Word and Your commandments from this day forward.*
>
> *Amen.*

By sincerely praying this, you are welcomed into God's family. You've been born again and your past will be remembered no more!

...if you confess with your mouth, "Jesus is Lord," and believe in your heart that God raised him from the dead, you will be saved.
– Romans 10:9

You have now accepted the perfect plan of God. He gives you the power through His son Jesus Christ to take on the divine nature and escape the desires of the enemy.

You are ready to begin earnestly praying for His will—and to accept His call.

His divine power has given us everything we need for life and godliness through our knowledge of him who called us by his own glory and goodness. Through these he has given us his very great and precious promises, so that through them you may participate in the divine nature and escape the corruption in the world caused by evil desires.
– 2 Peter 1:3-4

OBEY—AND GOD WILL DO THE REST

I remember when I decided to write my first book.

To be honest, I had no clue what I was doing; all I knew was God had placed a burden in my heart to write. So I sat down at my computer and began.

It was an amazing process. At first I was struggling to compose my thoughts, trying to snatch words out of thin air. But before long, the Lord began to pour concepts and ideas through me and my fingers were flying! I finished one chapter, two, then three. At the end of a few months the book was completed.

Before long, the Lord began to pour concepts and ideas through me and my fingers were flying!

Then the second miracle happened.

I knew it was going to take an investment to have the book published and I didn't have the funds. Yet, while I was praying, the Lord clearly spoke, assuring me:

> ***But my God shall supply all your need according to his riches in glory by Christ Jesus.***
> *– Philippians 4:19 KJV*

That very evening I walked into my church office and found a check sitting on the desk for exactly the amount needed. Attached was a note which read:

"We believe in your vision and we believe in you."

All I needed was to be obedient to God's call and He did the rest. I didn't even have to ask.

Remember, what God ordains, He sustains!

Jesus tells us:

> ***... do not worry about tomorrow,***
> ***for tomorrow will worry about itself.***
> *– Matthew 6:34*

The Lord is still letting us know the God we serve today will continue to meet our needs. All He asks is that we are faithful to His calling.

SOMEWHERE I BELONG

> ***From the day you were conceived, you began a personal journey to find yourself.***

From the day you were conceived, you began a personal journey to find yourself. Whether you are aware of it or not you have spent your entire life struggling to determine *who you are* and where you belong—a search for identity.

Maybe you have looked for the answer to come from your family or your friends. Some people search for meaning through social status or a higher level of education. It's a universal condition—everyone desperately seeks for a meaning of "self."

I have watched people try almost anything to achieve a sense of belonging. Sadly, many young people fall in with the wrong crowd just because someone reached out and became their friend. Then, because of peer pressure and the strong urge to be accepted, they found themselves in a downward cycle fueled by alcohol and drugs.

The question is the same for everyone: "Where do I belong?"

Just as the world was shaped—you too were created in the mind of God and you belong to Him.

There's only one source for the answer of *who you are* and *why you are here*—the God who gave you life.

After all, you don't belong to this world; it didn't create you and cannot give you true identity. Also, you did not create yourself, neither did your parents. They only facilitated the birth.

So where were you formed? Listen to me carefully when I tell you—just as the world was shaped—you too were created in the mind of God and you belong to Him.

For we are God's workmanship, created in Christ Jesus to do good works, which God prepared in advance for us to do.

– Ephesians 2:10

When you learn this truth you have unlocked the door to knowing yourself and finding your genuine identity. *All we have* and *all we are* is in Christ Jesus our Lord. Only by knowing Him can we truly know ourselves.

For in him we live, and move, and have our being...

—Acts 17:28

DON'T WRECK THE PLAN

One day my friend offered to let me drive his brand new Lexus convertible. "Here are the keys, Alan," he said, "Why don't you take it for a spin?"

My first thought was, "I really don't have $60,000 to spare, but then I decided, "Why not. I'm only going to live once!"

So I turned the key in the ignition, tapped on the accelerator and glided off. It was a strange feeling; driving someone else's luxury car down the road in an area I wasn't familiar with.

Then I began to worry: "Should I be driving this vehicle? What if I have a wreck?"

As a result I found myself being overly cautious.

"Should I be driving this vehicle? What if I have a wreck?"

Later, I thought about that driving experience and how it parallels life.

When we finally come to the realization we don't belong to ourselves and are the property of God, we will be much more careful with the choices we make. This is especially true when we become aware that our actions not only impact us personally, but affect the Father's plan for our future.

The same God you serve has your course charted. Why run the risk of making irresponsible choices that just might wreck His plan?

The apostle Paul asks:

Don't you know that you yourselves are God's temple and that God's Spirit lives in you?
– 1 Corinthians 3:16

When Jesus paid the ultimate price at Calvary He purchased our eternal salvation. And when we accept Him, the ownership papers are signed with His blood.

No longer are we part of the world system—a system that feeds off the wreckage of our lives.

We are now adopted into the family of God and belong to Him. No longer are we part of the world system—a system that feeds off the wreckage of our lives.

Praise God, we belong to One who lovingly protects and cares for His property.

IT'S ALL GOOD!

Many believe the misconception that just because they made a mistake they are not worthy of God's grace. Just a few lapses of their better judgment and they are ready to give up on themselves.

They need to know the only criteria necessary for

their future is their undying love for God. What matters is not failures or achievements, rather faithfulness to the Almighty and His purposes.

If you love the Lord, He will return the favor by turning your mistakes into miracles. When it is in God—it's all good!

Remember, He has a plan!

CHAPTER 4

THE POWER OF PURPOSE

When I was a child my heros were always people who had incredible abilities.

I thought Superman was the greatest. He was faster than a speeding bullet, more powerful than a locomotive and able to leap tall buildings in a single bound. You couldn't shoot him, burn him, crush him, cut him or run over him. His only weakness was *kryptonite*—and who had any of that stuff? Nobody I knew. He was unstoppable.

However, we all know Superman is fictional; he is not real.

A BURNING DESIRE

What if I told you that the right *purpose* could give you supernatural power?

If you don't believe me, think about the men and women who have overcome impossible odds to perform feats they could not accomplish in the natural.

- A injured pilot who crawls 20 miles in the snow to safety after his small plane crashes in the mountains of Idaho.
- A 110-pound mother who lifts the front of an automobile off the ground to free her trapped baby daughter.

What was the driving force that gave these people such power and determination? They had a burning desire—a purpose which gave them uncommon strength.

TOO LATE!

One day my grandfather was driving with his wife and newborn baby daughter from Greenville, South

Carolina to Akron, Ohio, where he was to preach a revival meeting.

It was late at night and the drive was long and arduous. His wife and little girl were fast asleep—and his eyes were getting drowsy. This was before cars had radios or air-conditioning, and prior to the time you could find a gas station on every corner to stop and revive yourself with a caffeine-laced beverage.

They were motoring through the foggy mountains of West Virginia when he started to doze off. By the time he came to and saw the bridge abutment it was too late to maneuver.

The rain was pouring down and they were stranded without another car in sight.

My grandfather's hands were bruised and broken and his neck was gashed open. His wife's face was covered in blood and their newborn baby had flown from behind the back seat into the windshield and was lying crumpled on the dashboard of the car with her head cut wide open.

As far as he knew, his wife and child were dead.

The rain was pouring down and they were stranded without another car in sight.

"PLEASE HAVE SOMEONE PRAY!"

As he climbed from the demolished car, my grandfather lifted his battered hand toward heaven. Holding his bleeding baby girl in the other arm, he felt himself begin to weaken. With his sight fading, he managed to raise his arm and cry, "Lord I have always prayed for others wherever you have sent me. Now, Lord, please have someone, somewhere pray for us."

They pulled her from the wreckage and said, "This one's dead."

Instantly he felt life flow back into his body and out of nowhere—on an isolated road with no houses in sight, at a time before cell phones and OnStar®—an ambulance appeared as if from nowhere.

My grandmother was lying unconscious when the paramedics arrived. They pulled her from the wreckage and said, "This one's dead."

As they lifted her into the ambulance, a man was standing there; he was dressed from head to toe in white and had blond curly hair. This person climbed in the back of the ambulance and stayed with my grandmother for the 40 mile ride to the hospital.

When they arrived at the emergency room, the mysterious passenger disappeared and was nowhere to be found. No one knew who he was or where he went.

You could never convince my grandfather of anything other than God had sent an angel to bring comfort to my injured grandmother.

The entire family should have died in the wreckage, but, praise God, a greater force saved their lives.

AWAKENED IN THE NIGHT

After the accident my grandparents got in touch with friends in Greenville and learned that members of the church had been awakened in the night and began praying for them—at the exact moment of the crash. Some people even called their pastor, asking, "Is everything okay with the Mushegans?"

Little did they know their prayers had been heard and had saved the lives of my grandparents.

I believe God sent both the ambulance and the angel. Why? Because Grandad had purpose in his life—as did his entire family.

It was the source of their protection.

AN UNSTOPPABLE FORCE

One day as I was meditating on God's Word, this phrase dropped into my spirit. I quickly wrote it down. "Stick with the winner. God has always been victorious and He will never, ever lose."

This began a whole new thought process as I realized as long as I was on working for God, on His team and following His purpose I could not be defeated.

I opened my Bible and read this scripture:

This is the purpose that is purposed upon the whole earth: and this is the hand that is stretched out upon all the nations. For the Lord of hosts has purposed and who shall disannul it? and his hand is stretched out, and who shall turn it back?

– Isaiah 14:26-27

The divine objective of God, what He has set in motion, cannot be turned back or broken apart. And when His will is at work within you, it's impossible for *you* to be stopped.

INTO THE DEN

Let me tell you about Daniel. After hearing the decree of King Darius that no one was to petition any god or man for thirty days, except for the king himself, defiant, Daniel still called on God.

With his curtains drawn back for the world to witness, Daniel prayed—despite the ruling. Then, when government officials rushed to inform the king of the disobedience, he was forced to throw Daniel in the den of lions.

King Darius rushed over to the den, expecting to see only the carcass of Daniel.

The next morning, at the first light of dawn, King Darius rushed over to the den, expecting to see only the carcass of Daniel. Finding none, in an anguished voice he asked:

> ***Daniel, servant of the living God, has your God, whom you serve continually, been able to rescue you from the lions?***
>
> *– Daniel 6:20*

He was surprised to hear a reply from this prayer warrior. Daniel answered:

> ***My God sent his angel, and he shut the mouths of the lions. They have not hurt me, because I was found innocent in his sight.***
> *– Daniel 6:22*

Untouched and unharmed, Daniel survived the night—then he was set free.

Why was this man such a relentless force? That's easy to answer. It was because he was moving in the will and purpose of the living Lord.

TALK ABOUT HEAT!

We see the same undaunted faith in the lives of the three Hebrew children—Shadrach, Meshach, and Abednego. They were thrown into a fiery furnace because they refused to bow down to the golden statue of King Nebuchadaezzar.

The royal monarch was so furious he commanded the furnace to be heated seven times hotter than its normal temperature. In fact, the men who cast them into the flames perished from the heat. Yet, to the king's surprise, the fire did not consume these three God-fearing, praying young men.

King Nebuchadanezzar jumped to his feet in amazement and asked his advisers:

Did not we cast three men bound into the midst of the fire? They answered and said unto the king, True, O king. He answered and said, Lo, I see four men loose, walking in the midst of the fire, and they have no hurt; and the form of the fourth is like the Son of God.

– Daniel 3:24-25

Shadrach, Meshach, and Abednego walked out of that burning caldron untouched. Their clothes did not reek of smoke, and the fire had not singed a hair on their head.

The reason they did not perish in a fiery death is because they were in the center of God's perfect will.

Their testimony could not be silenced.

YOU CAN'T STOP ME, SO GET OUT OF MY WAY!

When God is your partner, there are no

circumstances too great or no enemy too powerful.

A righteous man may have many troubles,
but the Lord delivers him from them all.
– Psalm 34:19

Regardless of what comes your way, when you are following the purpose of God, you cannot be deterred.

Regardless of what comes your way, when you are following the purpose of God you cannot be deterred.

Just before Jesus ascended to heaven, He uttered these final words—giving a preview of what believers could expect after His departure:

And these signs shall follow
them that believe; in my name shall
they cast out devils; they shall speak with
new tongues; They shall take up serpents; and
if they drink any deadly thing, it shall not hurt
them; they shall lay hands on the sick,
and they shall recover.
– Mark 16:17-18 KJV

Jesus was telling His disciples if they believe in His direction for their lives, nothing could stop them until their mission on earth was fulfilled.

When we have confidence God is always with us, there's not a roadblock or detour sign that will slow us down.

When we have confidence God is always with us, there's not a roadblock or detour sign that will slow us down. If we can't go through, we'll go around. But you will see us at the final destination!

A SURE CALLING

Read the psalms of David and you'll discover a man who had a certainty that could only come from God Himself. I get excited when I read his words:

For by thee I have run through a troop; and by my God I have leaped over a wall.
– Psalm 18:29

David developed this self-assurance as a young man while tending his father's sheep. The Lord had given him victory over a lion and a bear, so when it came time to face the giant Goliath he had learned to be reliant on God.

Most important, David was aware of his divine purpose since the time he was anointed by the prophet Samuel to be King of Judah.

That's why, even as a child, David began to behave like the king he was destined to be.

His brothers thought he was arrogant, but it was something more. David was called of God and he *knew* it!

It's Not Over 'Till It's Over!

The Bible teaches that God watches over His Word *"to perform it"* (Jeremiah 1:12). And how is the Word received?

So then faith cometh by hearing, and hearing by the word of God.
– Romans 10:17

This leaves me to conclude: the person who is *full of faith* is obviously *full of His Word.*

If the Lord is watching over His Word, then He must also be observing the place where His Word is sown.

This means when you are filled with scripture God

not only protects you—He is going to ensure that the Word you possess is going to come to life.

...being confident of this, that he who began a good work in you will carry it on to completion until the day of Christ Jesus.
– Philippians 1:6

Until God's promise for YOU has been completed, you are spiritually invincible. Jesus understood this when He said (concerning His life):

No one takes it from me, but I lay it down of my own accord. I have authority to lay it down and authority to take it up again. This command I received from my Father.
– John 10:18

Jesus knew He could not say "It is finished" until His Father commanded it to be over.

LET GOD ARISE!

When Jehovah rises up within you and you feel His presence and anointing, things change for the better.

As David writes:

May God arise, may his enemies be scattered; may his foes flee before him. As smoke is blown away by the wind, may you blow them away; as wax melts before the fire, may the wicked perish before God.

– Psalm 68:1-2

Don't be afraid of the obstacles you face. Since your Lord is bigger than any foe, you will have victory—the enemy will run like the coward he is.

- When God arose on behalf of Moses the sea parted.
- When God arose in Samson he accomplished heroic feats of strength.
- When God arose in David he was able to slay Goliath with only a slingshot.

Arise, shine, for your light has come, and the glory of the Lord rises upon you.

– Isaiah 60:1

How does God arise? Does He appear with the sun of a new day? No. God will arrive the moment you *allow* Him to fill you with His presence.

...for it is God who works in you to will and to act according to his good purpose.
– Philippians 2:13

When God's purpose comes alive—you begin to shine! All your hidden talents and abilities rise to the surface. This is possible because it is not your strength at work, but the power of God working in you.

When God's purpose comes alive—you begin to shine!

Big problems require a big answer. Let God be God!

YOUR PROVIDER

Are you ready for more good news? When you are involved in God's plan, you have God's *provision.*

Think of how the Lord miraculously supplied the children of Israel in the desert:

- He didn't let their clothes wear out for 40 years! (Deuteronomy 29:5).
- Their shoes didn't fall apart! (v.5).

- They were fed with heavenly food (Exodus 16:35).
- When they were thirsty He caused water to flow from a rock (Nehemiah 9:15).

GOD'S GOT YOUR BACK!

It seems obvious to me the Lord knows how to take care of His people! He will stand on your behalf and fight for you. As I tell young people: "God's got your back!"

"If someone wants to mess with you, they'll have to go through me first!"

Have you ever had a friend say, "If someone wants to mess with you, they'll have to go through me first!"?

That is a nice sentiment, but their protection can't compare with having the force of Almighty God on your side.

There's even better news! When you are faithful to the Lord and following His purpose, *your* enemies become *His* enemies. As a result, new doors are going to open and no one will be able to keep you from walking through them.

THE LOVE CONNECTION

The reason God performs and provides on your behalf is because of a love relationship. He declares:

I love those who love me,
and those who seek me find me.
– Proverbs 8:17

If you have given your heart to His Son, nothing can drive a wedge between you and your Heavenly Father. It's a love that results in hope, strength, health, wisdom and understanding.

Who shall separate us from the love of Christ? Shall trouble or hardship or persecution or famine or nakedness or danger or sword?...For I am convinced that neither death nor life, neither angels nor demons, neither the present nor the future, nor any powers, neither height nor depth, nor anything else in all creation, will be able to separate us from the love of God that is in Christ Jesus our Lord.
– Romans 8:35,38-39

I recently heard a man give this excuse for the breakup in a relationship: "Oh, we fell out of love."

That comment doesn't pass the test of logic. I don't believe he fell out of love, rather, he was never in love in the first place!

According to the Bible, real love endures all things:

Love is patient, love is kind. It does not envy, it does not boast, it is not proud. It is not rude, it is not self-seeking, it is not easily angered, it keeps no record of wrongs. Love does not delight in evil but rejoices with the truth. It always protects, always trusts, always hopes, always perseveres. Love never fails.

– 1 Corinthians 13:4-8

THE POWER OF AGREEMENT

Just as love requires the participation of two parties, so does God's purpose. It is between you and Him—and being united is a requirement.

Do two walk together unless they have agreed to do so?

– Amos 3:3

"Going against the flow" doesn't cut it when you are dealing with life and death, heaven and hell, even giving and receiving.

In football, what good is an all-pro quarterback if he doesn't have a receiver to catch the ball? It takes two—one to pass and one to receive.

The Bible tells us:

> ***But as many as received him, to them gave he power to become the sons of God, even to them that believe on his name.***
>
> *—John 1:12*

How can we line up with the Father's plan when we are not on the same page and headed in the wrong direction? Saul learned this lesson on the road to Damascus. Jonah had a "whale of an experience" trying to flee to Tarshish.

It's only when we are in full agreement with God's program we will know His peace.

Jesus says:

If anyone loves me, he will obey my teaching. My Father will love him, and we will come to him and make our home with him.

– John 14:23

What must I be in agreement with? His Word, His will, His Spirit and His Son.

Before the crucifixion Jesus was talking about both His relationship with God and with you and me when He said:

I have given them the glory that you gave me, that they may be one as we are one.

– John 17:22

MISSION POSSIBLE

In my teens I came to the realization I could never make it on my own. I desperately needed the Lord in every aspect and activity. And today, without His purpose stamped on my heart I'm hopelessly adrift—like a sailboat with no breeze.

What a difference God's guidance makes—the possibilities are limitless. Here's what I have found: the Lord will never ask you to do something He will not give you the ability to perform.

The mission God has for you is one you already have the potential talent and skill to carry out. And what you are lacking He will supernaturally supply.

How do I know this is true? It comes directly from God's Son. Jesus says:

> ***With man this is impossible, but with God all things are possible.***
>
> *– Matthew 19:26*

Do we believe the Lord truly means it when He says "all things"? If so we will no longer walk in fear, knowing God is in control of our past, present, and future.

The problem most people face is allowing past failures to control their thoughts. Instead of having the "mind of God," they permit their own thinking to dictate what they can and cannot do.

The problem most people face is allowing past failures to control their thoughts.

This is the direct opposite of Jesus telling us "all things are possible."

Listen to the skeptics and they'll use words such as

"It *seems* impossible," or "It *feels* impossible." However, we can't make decisions based on our emotions. They will always deceive us.

Instead of looking at the size of your problem, look at the greatness of God.

HOLD ON TO HOPE

Some allow the smallest issues to freeze them dead in their tracks. If a person looks at them the wrong way you would think the world had come to an end. Or if their boss levels a criticism that seems too personal, they're ready to resign.

Instead of looking at the size of your problem, look at the greatness of God.

If "all things" are working for our good, why don't we take a deep breath and see our circumstances from God's vantage point. Could it be the Lord wants these conflicts to help us build relationships that will be "tested by fire" and strengthened.

Even if you lose your job, don't be afraid. God has a reason for everything—He has something far better in mind for your future.

Let us hold unswervingly to the hope we profess, for he who promised is faithful.

– Hebrews 10:23

CHOOSE TO ACCEPT THE MISSION

For God's purpose to become reality you must first make a decision to accept God's calling.

Here is what He told Joshua:

No one will be able to stand up against you all the days of your life. As I was with Moses, so I will be with you; I will never leave you nor forsake you. Be strong and courageous, because you will lead these people to inherit the land I swore to their forefathers to give them....Be careful to obey all the law my servant Moses gave you; do not turn from it to the right or to the left, that you may be successful wherever you go.

– Joshua 1:5-7

If God makes a promise, He will do it. Who are we to question?

Just as God spoke to Joshua He is speaking to you and me: "You can go as far as you are *willing* to go."

Once, when Jesus was ministering:

> ***...two blind men followed him, calling out, "Have mercy on us, Son of David! " When he had gone indoors, the blind men came to him, and he asked them "Do you believe that I am able to do this?" "Yes, Lord," they replied." Then he touched their eyes and said, "According to your faith will it be done to you," and their sight was restored.***
>
> *– Matthew 9:27-30*

These "men of vision" received *according to their faith!*

GO FOR IT!

God is looking for those who will be faithful, loyal and *aggressive* in the fulfillment of the mission. Instead of standing on the outskirts, go for it with boldness!

Jesus gives us the marching orders:

I tell you the truth, whatever you bind on earth will be bound in heaven, and whatever you loose on earth will be loosed in heaven.

– Matthew 18:18

If you want to claim the Lord's promise, stop complaining of what you don't have, and claim what God says is yours!

It's the only way you will be able to say, "Mission accomplished!"

Chapter 5

A Spiritual Matrix

The movie, *The Matrix,* is about a man being chosen to be the "one" who delivers all of humanity from a computer-simulated world.

Bear with me while I set the scene.

The character Neo, played by Keanu Reeves, is a digital whiz who finds out his life is more than he imagined. When he takes a trip "down the rabbit hole," or *out* of the matrix, he comes face to face with a harsh reality. He awakens in the real world, which is being controlled by machines, and he sees all the other humans who are plugged into the matrix, trapped in a cocoon-like state.

Soon, Neo realizes his entire life has been a dream, and that he has spent his existence caught up in the matrix.

After adapting to his new environment he is taught by Morphious how to survive in the matrix. Morphious then tells Neo the prophecy of the "one" who would deliver Zion—the last remaining city in the real world populated by human beings.

When he was ready to go back into the matrix he was taken by Morphious to the Oracle, a woman who could see the future. She tells him "being 'the one' is like falling in love either you know it or you don't."

By the end of the movie Neo realizes he is *the one* and that he has the power to manipulate the matrix.

THE BULLETS FALL

It is this realization of *self* which gives him the ability to defeat the agents who are policing the matrix to stop Zion from releasing more human minds. To me, this is the pivotal scene that really stands out in the film.

The agents try to shoot him and he simply says to the bullets, "No" while raising his hand. The bullets immediately stop in mid air and fall to the ground. Neo had found his true self and learned his purpose was to save the city of Zion from the mind-controlling machines.

WHAT IS REAL?

As I watched this Hollywood epic, I could not help seeing the comparison to the real world.

In many respects, life is like living in the matrix. We see the natural, physical things we are going through as being more tangible than the spirit realm—when actually the opposite is true.

> ***If we want to be free to reach our God-ordained destiny, we must revolutionize the way we think.***

If we want to be free to reach our God-ordained destiny, we must revolutionize the way we think. Let me express it as succinctly as I know how: *the spirit is more real than the natural because the Spirit of God created the physical things we see and experience.*

MAKING A STAND

You are not limited to your "earthly mind" because through the Spirit we have taken on the mind of God.

When we live and operate in the Spirit we can control natural things. For example, just as Neo was able to repel the bullets we are able to ward off the attack of the enemy.

Let me remind you of this important verse we discussed in Chapter Four. Jesus declared:

I will give you the keys of the kingdom of heaven; whatever you bind on earth will be bound in heaven, and whatever you loose on earth will be loosed in heaven.

– Matthew 16:19

It's absolutely mind-boggling, yet true. Through the Spirit of God we have the awesome power and ability to stop floundering and to make a committed stand against our problems.

When we realize the power is *within us,* all we are asked to do is say "NO" and the enemy has to depart.

Resist the devil, and he will flee from you.

– James 4:7

By taking this spiritual stand, the things which once

tormented us will harm us no more.

CONTROLLING CIRCUMSTANCES

Don't become seduced and caught up in the deception and lies swirling around you. Otherwise you will miss out on the greatness of your God-given potential. Never forget you have been chosen and hand-picked by the Lord. Furthermore, when we are in Christ, our minds have been freed from this world.

Just as important, we have been called to liberate the minds of others who have also been deceived by giving them the message of the Savior. This is God's plan— and you and I have been chosen to carry it out.

We have been called to liberate the minds of others who have also been deceived by giving them the message of the Savior.

It is *only* when you realize the power the Almighty has placed within that you can control your circumstances and stop the work of the enemy. You have the authority through Jesus Christ to say "no" and watch the enemy's artillery fall to the ground.

TAKING CONTROL

There is a marked difference between a citizen of heaven and one who is bound by this earth. Here's what scripture tells us:

> ***Therefore if any man be in Christ, he is a new creature: old things are passed away; behold, all things are become new.***
>
> *– 2 Corinthians 5:17 KJV*

When we are "born again," we are not birthed of this world, but of the Holy Spirit. We are adopted into the family of God and now—through the blood of Jesus—carry His genetic code.

When we are "born again," we are not birthed of this world, but of the Holy Spirit.

This is why, as *sons* and *daughters* of God, we have His *authority* through Jesus Christ.

Since God created natural things, we as His offspring have dominion over those same objects. This was established in the Garden of Eden, when the Creator declared:

Let us make man in our image, after our likeness: and let them have dominion...over all the earth...

– Genesis 1:26 KJV

This granted our *rights* to have control—and God works within the parameters we set as His children. This is how He arranged "the order of things" from the beginning. And this being true, the Creator is bound by His Word to work through man to bring about His kingdom upon the earth.

Only the Lord can tell you why He did it this way, but in His infinite wisdom and divine plan He chose us, His children, to bring about His purpose and to take control.

HOW BOUNDARIES ARE SET

If it is true that God can only work within boundaries, then how is it that we set these limits? We establish them by our faith in Him.

When we have belief and expectation in a specific area, that's where the Lord moves. In other words, God operates within the confines of our faith.

Certainly, the Almighty is an unlimited all-powerful

being, but He chooses to operate in in the realm of our faith to bring about His power and glory in our lives.

Now can you see why the world is waiting for the sons and daughters of God to arise and take authority? It has *always* been the Father's plan for His children to rule and reign in the earth.

The creation waits in eager expectation for the sons of God to be revealed.

– Romans 8:19

Everything we see—both the creature and the creation—is a byproduct of the Spirit. Therefore He is waiting on those who are *spiritual* to take control.

Everything we see—both the creature and the creation—is a byproduct of the Spirit.

The *same Spirit* which formed all things is the *same Spirit* who is the creative force within us. This is why we can "call those things that are not as though they were."

When you speak as a child of God all of creation must respond. The whole world is waiting on you to arise and allow the Great Jehovah to move.

ARE YOU REALLY THE ONE?

When Jesus came on the scene and miracles began to take place, the people were filled with awe and praised God. They exclaimed:

> ***"A great prophet has appeared among us...God has come to help his people." This news about Jesus spread throughout Judea and the surrounding country.***
>
> *– Luke 7:16-17*

John the Baptist sent out his followers to ask Jesus,

> ***Are you the one who was to come, or should we expect someone else?***
>
> *– Luke 7:20*

I believe John always knew Jesus was the Messiah, but while he was in jail knowing he was about to die he wanted his own disciples to find out for themselves that Jesus was "The One" by hearing it from His own mouth.

Jesus knew He was sent by God, so He had no

hesitancy to operate with the purpose and destiny given by His Heavenly Father.

Here is how He replied to the messengers of John:

Go back and report to John what you have seen and heard: The blind receive sight, the lame walk, those who have leprosy are cured, the deaf hear, the dead are raised, and the good news is preached to the poor.

– Luke 7:22

Jesus was saying, "You will know I am the One by the works I do." It is also why He told them, "Tell John what you have seen and heard."

WHAT DO WE BELIEVE?

The power we have been given is the power of choice:

- Are we the ones God is going to use for His Glory?
- Are we the ones that have been given great purpose?

- Are we the children of the Most High God?

The answer to these questions is that we are only what we *believe* ourselves to be.

As Christians, we have been given the keys to the kingdom, and now it's all about faith and choice. Do we believe Jesus to be the Christ? Do we believe His power to be at work in us? Do we believe what we bind on earth will be bound in heaven?

The keys rest in your hand! It's up to you to determine how far you will go—and whether you will allow the Lord to help you fulfill His purpose.

Jesus says, *"...many are called, but few are chosen"* (Matthew 22:14).

What is the reason for this? Only a handful of the called choose to walk in their calling. They follow the lure of this world instead of the call and purpose of God for their lives. Are you *the one?* The choice is yours.

IT'S YOUR DECISION

We have been declared a *"chosen generation, a royal priesthood"* (1 Peter 2:9), but as human beings we have to *choose* to be a part of what God has designed. You see, the Lord will not *force* His purpose on you. He is bound by His Word and has created us as free moral agents with the right to accept or reject life or death.

Where do you stand? What is your decision?

CHAPTER 6

THE DYNAMITE WITHIN

Earlier, I shared with you my childhood fascination with Superman. However, he was just one of my "super-heros."

I also loved anything to do with characters such as Spiderman or the Incredible Hulk—movies, comic books or action figures. It drove my parents nuts!

I can still remember tying towels around my neck and jumping off high tables thinking I could somehow fly—or I would pretend to possess a special power only I knew about.

YOUR SECRET STRENGTH

As I grew older I came to the realization I really *did* have a super power, but it wasn't a creation of Hollywood. The person who, on the outside, has a mild mannered demeanor (such as reporter Clark Kent) *can* know a power which turns them into super men and women.

You have a mighty force within you just waiting to be unleashed. It is a potential yet to be uncovered.

You know what I'm talking about. The secret is receiving the power of the Holy Spirit.

YOUR UNCOVERED POTENTIAL

It's true! You have a mighty force within you just waiting to be unleashed. It is a potential yet to be uncovered.

The apostle Paul says:

> ***...we have this treasure in earthen vessels, that the excellency of the power may be of God, and not of us.***
>
> *– 2 Corinthians 4:7*

The seed of this force has been in you since the

beginning of your existence and ignites at the very moment you accept Jesus Christ into your heart.

STIR UP THE GIFT

This seed was actually placed within you by God Himself *before* you were born, but it will remain buried until you have a revelation of Jesus Christ and His Spirit which works in you. This power deep inside cannot be seen until faith in you is activated and it allows your talents and calling to become apparent.

This power deep inside cannot be seen until faith in you is activated and allows your talents and calling to become apparent.

Paul told Timothy:

Wherefore I put thee in remembrance that thou stir up the gift of God, which is in thee by the putting on of my hands.

– 2 Timothy 1:6 KJV

We are able to bring these gifts to the surface when we allow our faith in Jesus to trigger the seed of power within us.

WHAT A CROP!

Jesus said our faith in God resembles a tiny seed, and when it is planted can grow into a tree which produces a bountiful harvest of fruit.

The seed He described:

...came up, grew and produced a crop, multiplying thirty, sixty, or even a hundred times.
– Mark 4:8

The point of the parable is to remind us when we activate the kernel of greatness through faith, our gifts will be made manifest.

When we activate the kernel of greatness through faith, our gifts will be made manifest.

"IS IT IN YOU?"

Gatorade, the high-energy drink, once ran a series of commercials with two athletes competing against each another. One athlete would be taking a gulp of Gatorade and the other just drank tap water.

Amazingly, the person who was full of Gatorade was sweating out the color of the drink through his pores during the competition—while the fellow consuming only water couldn't keep up with the Gatorade athlete. He would always collapse, exhausted.

The slogan for the ad campaign and string of commercials was: "Is It In You?"

Here was the implication: Gatorade gives you an edge over your competitors.

"GOT GOD?"

There is also another popular energy drink on the market called Red Bull. Their slogan is "Red Bull Gives You Wings." It implies when you drink their product you will become more alert, mentally aware and have the ability to physically perform at a greater level.

When you have the Lord in you, you become more than a conqueror—someone who is built to outlast any situation or crisis.

Or maybe you remember the ads that ballyhooed: "Milk it does the body good, and "Got Milk?"

My question to you may sound grammatically incorrect, but I'll ask it anyway: "Got God?"

When you have the Lord *in* you, you become *more* than a conqueror—someone who is built to outlast any situation or crisis because the power of Jesus

Christ resides within.

SPIRITUAL FUEL

The Lord may have created us with a special purpose, but we will never complete the intended mission until we have the power—the spiritual fuel which makes us run!

Every person who goes without food eventually gets hungry. And if their nutritional depravation lasts too long their mind and body will shut down.

It is the same with the cars we drive or the planes we fly in; these machines require fuel to reach their destination. A car may have all the amenities money can buy, but without gas it's not going to perform what it was designed to do—be a mode of transportation to get you from point A to point B.

WHAT'S IN YOUR TANK?

The Lord may have created us with a specific purpose, but we will never complete the intended mission until we have the power—the spiritual fuel—which makes us *run!*

Jesus tells us:

Man does not live on bread alone, but on every word that comes from the mouth of God.
– Matthew 4:4

The energy we require is the Word of God which activates our faith. Again, the Bible clearly states:

So then faith cometh by hearing, and hearing by the word of God.
– Romans 10:17

Jesus also declared:

If ye abide in me, and my words abide in you, ye shall ask what ye will, and it shall be done unto you.
– John 15:7 KJV

When we fill the tank of our lives with the Word of God, faith starts our engine churning and "all things become possible." We can now be driven with divine energy.

It's Explosive!

I am not ashamed of the gospel, because it is

the power of God for the salvation of everyone who believes: first for the Jew, then for the Gentile.
– Romans 1:16

This is one of my favorite Bible verses. The Greek translation for the word *power* used here is *dunamis,* which is: "as a great force or an abundance of might, strength, or ability."

It also more specifically means *miraculous power.* From *dunamis* is derived our English word "dynamite."

These ingredients blast apart any negative thoughts or barriers I need to break through.

This verse is the message of the Gospel—which is the truth about Jesus Christ—and contains an explosive element which transforms and changes everyone who believes.

Personally, this faith gives me *dynamite power* which not only allows me to receive my salvation, but is also the source of my unquenchable passion to live out the same gospel, Word, and truth I have received.

These ingredients blast apart any negative thoughts or barriers I need to break through.

I also like to quote Romans 1:16 this way: "I am

not ashamed of the word of God in me because it is the power I require to live the abundant life and be like Christ."

SUPERNATURAL POWER

The Almighty is "all Super" and we are "all natural." It is only when His *super* is united with our *natural* we can generate supernatural power.

If God is the omnipotent Creator of the universe and He works and lives in me, I also possess that same creative power.

If God is the omnipotent Creator of the Universe and He works and lives in me, I also possess that same creative power.

Listen to these words of Jesus:

All authority in heaven and on earth has been given to me.
– Matthew 28:18

From scripture we know what was given to Christ. But what about you and me? What has the Father granted to us?

TIME FOR AN EXAM

Let me give you a test. Look at the next three verses and see how many seconds it takes you to find two adjoining words that show up in each verse. Ready, set, go!

1.

...for it is God who works in you to will and to act according to his good purpose.

– Philippians 2:13

2.

...Christ in you, the hope of glory.

– Colossians 1:27

3.

You, dear children, are from God and have overcome them, because the one who is in you is greater than the one who is in the world.

– 1 John 4:4

How long did it take you find the answer?

The two words appearing in all three of the above scriptures are "IN YOU".

Did you know these words appear together exactly 60 times in the King James version of the Bible? I think

God must be trying to tell us something!

Here's the message the Lord wants us to absorb: if God is *in you* and the power of His son Jesus is *in you* then *all power* must also be yours because "all power" is in Jesus.

Don't you know that you yourselves are God's temple and that God's Spirit lives in you?
– 1 Corinthians 3:16

Hallelujah! Since you contain God's *dunamis* you are *super*-natural!

CHAPTER 7

YOUR TOOL BOX

One night as I was teaching at our Atlanta youth ministry, *Full Turn,* I desperately wanted to show how each person was unique and how every one of them was created with purpose.

Hundreds of teenagers were present.

The Lord inspired me to present this simple illustration. I had a big red toolbox brought out and placed on the stage. Next, I began to pull out each tool and explain its function.

I could see the young people thinking, "What on earth does this have to do with anything?"

Then I began to emphasize how, "These tools are not a 'set' unless they are all present, in good working condition and functioning together. Only then can they build something worthwhile."

I could see a glimmer of understanding starting to reflect on their faces. The young people were beginning to understand where I was headed with this "tool visual."

I continued, "Just like the tools, we are each created for a specific purpose. We all have a one-of-a-kind assignment we were designed to do, yet we need to link up with each other's purpose to build something magnificent for God."

They began to grasp the connection. It is only when we combine our efforts to form the complete "set"—the body of Christ—does God's Kingdom advance.

PICK UP THE HAMMER!

Let's take a look at what Paul the apostle says concerning this truth:

> ***Just as each of us has one body with many members, and these members do not all have the same function, so in Christ we who are many form one body, and each member belongs to all the others.***
>
> *– Romans 12:4-5*

You cannot construct a house using only a hammer or just a screwdriver. Every tool in the box has a specific function, yet it takes *all* the tools to build something worthy of our toil and effort.

God is the Master Builder and He is fashioning His Church. Each of us are tool's in the Carpenter's hands.

God is the Master Builder and He is fashioning His Church.

However, If we were all the same we could never get the job done. Who needs forty teachers and no prayer warriors? It is in our diversity we are able to advance the Kingdom and meet spiritual needs.

BODY-BUILDING

Read carefully the words Paul wrote to the believers at Ephesus:

It was he who gave some to be apostles,
some to be prophets, some to be evangelists,
and some to be pastors and teachers, to prepare
God's people for works of service, so that the body
of Christ may be built up until we all reach unity

in the faith and in the knowledge of the Son of God and become mature, attaining to the whole measure of the fullness of Christ.

– Ephesians 4:11-13

Then we will no longer be infants, tossed back and forth by the waves, and blown here and there by every wind of teaching and by the cunning and craftiness of men in their deceitful scheming. Instead, speaking the truth in love, we will in all things grow up into him who is the head, that is, Christ. From him the whole body, joined and held together by every supporting ligament, grows and builds itself up in love, as each part does its work.

– Ephesians 4:14-16

This passage proves we all have purpose that can only be fulfilled as members in the body of believers. I have heard my father say many times, "There are no Lone Rangers in the Church of Jesus Christ." We all need each other—it is the only way we can be complete in our mission.

REALIZE YOUR FUNCTION

Just as a symphony doesn't sound balanced with only a tympani and a trombone, we need an entire orchestra to harmonize and make beautiful music—and to function in the purpose for which we were created.

This is what the apostle Paul had to say on the matter. It's a lengthy passage, yet extremely important:

The body is a unit, though it is made up of many parts; and though all its parts are many, they form one body. So it is with Christ. For we were all baptized by one Spirit into one body—whether Jews or Greeks, slave or free —and we were all given the one Spirit to drink. Now the body is not made up of one part but of many.

– 1 Corinthians 12:12-14

If the foot should say, "Because I am not a hand, I do not belong to the body," it would not for that reason cease to be part of the body. And if the ear should say, "Because I am not an eye, I do not belong to the body," it would not for that reason cease to be part of the body. If the whole body were an eye, where would the sense of hearing be? If the whole body were an ear, where would the sense of smell be?

– v v.15-17

But in fact God has arranged the parts in the body, every one of them, just as he wanted them to be. If they were all one part, where would the body be? As it is, there are many parts, but one body. The eye cannot say to the hand, "I don't need you!" And the head cannot say to the feet, "I don't need you!"

– v v.18-21

On the contrary, those parts of the body that seem to be weaker are indispensable, and the parts that we think are less honorable we treat with special honor. And the parts that are unpresentable are treated with special modesty, while our presentable parts need no special treatment. But God has combined the members of the body and has given greater honor to the parts that lacked it, so that there should be no division in the body, but that its parts should have equal concern for each other. If one part suffers, every part suffers with it; if one part is honored, every part rejoices with it. Now you are the body of Christ, and each one of you is a part of it.

– v v. 22-27

"WHAT KIND OF TOOL AM I?"

What were you created to do? This question is vital because you will never be truly fulfilled until you find your perfect place in God's service.

It is He who made you and only through His Spirit can you find the answer. However, let me give you some practical steps to help you discover your role.

Ask yourself:

- "What are some of my natural talents and abilities?
- "What activities do I truly love to be involved in"
- What is my true passion–the thing I want to do more than anything in this world?
- What makes me feel alive and fulfilled?

Be honest with yourself. Do you recognize the real you?

After all, a hammer could never call itself a screwdriver. A wrench could never assume to be a measuring tape. Don't think of the things you *wish* you could do. Determine what you know you could accomplish if given the opportunity—those abilities which come naturally.

What are the observations others have made concerning your potential? Are you a good writer? Can you sing? Are you a whiz with numbers? Are you proficient as an organizer?

Determine what you know you could accomplish if given the opportunity.

Don't assume your calling is to sing if you can't carry a tune in a bucket! If you can answer these questions truthfully this could be the start of something big!

Chapter 8

Two Roads

After watching one of our television programs, a young woman sent an e-mail with this question: "If God has a plan and purpose for everyone, then why do people die and go to hell? Doesn't He care about us?"

It was an excellent question, but rather than giving my personal opinion, I turned immediately to the Word of God:

> ***The Lord is not slow in keeping his promise, as some understand slowness. He is patient with you, not wanting anyone to perish, but everyone to come to repentance.***
>
> *– 2 Peter 3:9*

I also found the answer I needed in this passage from the Old Testament:

For I know the thoughts I think toward you, saith the Lord, thoughts of peace, and not of evil, to give to you an expected end.
–Jeremiah 29:11 KJV

The New International Version of the Bible translates the verse: "I know the plans I have for you."

Both of these scriptures show us God has our best interest in mind and lets us know that hell is not our God-given destination. The Lord's design for His children is one of peace, not destruction.

Remember, God created us to take authority and dominion over the earth. We are His inheritance and He loves us.

Let's read the words of the most quoted scripture in the Bible:

For God so loved the world, that he gave his only begotten Son, that whosoever believeth in him should not perish, but have everlasting life.
–John 3:16 KJV

This was spoken by Jesus Himself, and if you'll read the next verse you will have an insight into how He feels about punishment.

For God sent not his son into the world to condemn the world; but that the world through him might be saved.
–John 3:17 KJV

To me, it is clear. The Lord does not want to condemn us to hell. Rather, He desires a loving relationship. However, the phrase in verse 17, "might be saved" lets us know salvation is not automatic—it requires a choice.

To me, it is clear. The Lord does not want to send us to hell.

WHICH PATH?

There are two roads: one leads to eternal life with God, the other to death, and a place of "outer darkness."

According to the Word, God longs for every human being to find *His* path and *His* purpose so they will know hope for the future and walk in their divine calling.

Let's go back to the young woman's question. "If God has a plan and purpose for everyone, then why do people die and go to hell?"

It's all wrapped up in one word: choice.

As the Bible tells us:

There is a way that seems right to a man, but in the end it leads to death.
– Proverbs 14:12

If we live for "feel good" carnal desires we're writing our own death certificate. But in Christ we become a brand new creation. The contrast is night and day!

Let me encourage you to study Romans 8 on the subject of the law of sin and death. In Paul's letter to the believers at Rome, he writes:

Those who live according to the sinful nature have their minds set on what that nature desires; but those who live in accordance with the Spirit have their minds set on what the Spirit desires.

The mind of sinful man is death, but the mind controlled by the Spirit is life and peace...
– Romans 8:5-6

When we accept Christ we also receive the gift of His purpose—which is everlasting peace. However, just as God has constructed a road, so has the enemy. Jesus compares each, telling us to:

Enter through the narrow gate. For wide is the gate and broad is the road that leads to destruction, and many enter through it. But small is the gate and narrow the road that leads to life, and only a few find it.
– Matthew 7:13-14

"THAT APPLE SURE LOOKS GOOD!"

In His infinite wisdom, God allows us to call our own shots and make the final decisions.

In His infinite wisdom, God allows us to call our own shots and make the final decisions.

This has been His operating procedure from the beginning when Adam and Eve were placed in the garden with two trees: (1) the Tree of Life and (2) the Tree of the Knowledge of Good and Evil.

In this land of abundance, the Lord laid down only one rule: they were not to eat the fruit of the second tree. Yet man chose to disobey—and we are still paying the price for the bite of that apple!

Now, thousands of years later, we continue to have the power over our own destiny. Which road will we choose?

READ THE STREET SIGNS

Life's highways are clearly marked: one has a street sign called "Blessing," the other is labeled "Cursing."

God says:

This day I call heaven and earth as witnesses against you that I have set before you life and death, blessings and curses. Now choose life, so that you and your children may live.

– Deuteronomy 30:19

Most people shrug their shoulders and put their fate in the hands of God, thinking life is out of their control.

Nothing could be further from the truth. The Creator leaves the decision making entirely up to us—and, for better or for worse, we have to live with the ultimate consequences.

Unfortunately, people constantly blame God for their own foolish decisions:

- They eat the wrong foods and blame God when they have a heart attack.
- They shirk their work responsibilities and blame God because they got fired.
- They drive like maniacs and curse God when they have a wreck.

Friend, it's not the Lord's fault when you choose to drive the wrong direction on a one-way street. After all, you're behind the wheel. Right decisions are the result of taking personal responsibility.

Right decisions are the result of taking personal responsibility.

The best way to get back on track is to pick up a copy of the Father's roadmap—His Holy Word. We know it is a lamp unto our feet (Psalm 119:105), and when we obey it, our behavior changes.

The psalmist writes:

I have kept my feet from every evil path so that I might obey your word.
– Psalm 119:101

STAY ON COURSE

Choosing the right path and *staying* on course are two separate issues. Just because you have followed God's way does not mean you won't be sidetracked.

There's an old southern tune called "Life's Railway to Heaven." It includes these words:

Watch the hills, the curves the tunnels,
Never falter, never fail.
Keep your hand upon the throttle,
And your eye upon the rail.

Life is riddled with unexpected twists and turns, and unless you heed God's voice you'll wind up in the ditch!

Stay tuned and listen to the Spirit—your Guide.

"LITTLE MUD CHURCH"

Since I started banging the spoon on my highchair, I've always been into making music—even though my folks just thought it was "noise" in those early years.

However, it seemed to come naturally. Almost

every person in our family has a musical talent.

As I grew older I was introduced to the creative and performance side of the art. Then, at nineteen, with my younger brother, Aram, I started a Christian rock band called "Little Mud Church."

We'd practice by the hour and play for any ears who would listen—whether they paid us or not. Most didn't!

One day an experienced music manager heard us and said, "We really like your sound and think we can take you to the next level."

"We really like your sound and think we can take you to the next level."

The "next level" to them wasn't just Christian music but a crossover band who could really climb up in the mainstream charts.

Now in my early twenties, I envisioned fame—huge concerts, number one hits, a tour bus, the works! The very idea of having our music heard by millions was rather heady!

THE ULTIMATE DECISION

As I always do when faced with a major choice, I turned to my dad for his advice.

"Alan, he told me, the ultimate decision is up to

you, but remember this. Musicians come a dime a dozen—and there are thousands of songwriters and bands in this world who are able to take the stage and perform."

Then he looked me in the eyes and got straight to the point. "Son," he continued, "you are faced with a serious choice of whether you are going 'sell out' and be like everyone else— and start playing in the bars and clubs on your way up. Are you going to perform for the applause of men, or will you use you music talent for a higher purpose?"

That day I made a crucial decision. I committed myself totally to the Lord and determined I would become "God's man"—and follow wherever He led.

Thank the Lord, I chose the right road. Today my band performs every Monday night to hundreds of teens at *Full Turn*—and to an audience of millions via television worldwide three times a week. Most important, thousands of young people have found Christ as a result of that decision.

WHERE'S THE EXIT?

I remember the day "Little Mud Church" was

scheduled to play at the Trinity Broadcasting Network studios in Hendersonville, Tennessee. As we approached the Intertstate exit near TBN, we started screaming, "This is the exit. Hurry—get off!" but our bus driver sailed right on by because he was talking to a band member and not paying attention to the road signs.

On your spiritual journey don't become distracted. It would be a shame to miss the right exit to your reward!

Listen to the Lord as He says:

> ***Obey my voice, and I will be your God, and ye shall be my people: and walk ye in all the ways that I have commanded you, that it may be well unto you.***
>
> *– Jeremiah 7:23 KJV*

BREAK THE CYCLE

In unfamiliar territory it's so easy to get lost and find yourself wandering around in circles. This happened to the children of Israel.

Moses led two million people out of Egypt on their way to their Promised Land. They began the exodus with strength and expectation —including the spoils of their captors. But instead of a straight highway to Canaan, they ended up roaming in the wilderness for 40 years.

They kept going around in circles because they didn't know how to break the cycle of committing and complaining, worshiping and whining.

The reason the children of Israel never walked into the "land of milk and honey" is because they never truly believed they could.

I've met people just like this who begin on the right track, but somewhere along the line they settle for second best.

The reason the children of Israel did not walk into the "land of milk and honey" is because they never truly *believed* they could—it was their choice.

Even at the end of their journey, when Moses sent twelve spies to check out the land of Canaan, ten of the twelve returned with a negative report, including stories of "giants in the land." One spy complained, *"We seemed like grasshoppers in our own eyes, and we looked the same to them"* (Numbers 13:33).

The rumor mill started buzzing and fear swept

through the camp. The Bible records:

That night all the people of the community raised their voices and wept aloud. All the Israelites grumbled against Moses and Aaron, and the whole assembly said to them, "If only we had died in Egypt! Or in this desert! Why is the Lord bringing us to this land only to let us fall by the sword? Our wives and children will be taken as plunder. Wouldn't it be better for us to go back to Egypt?" And they said to each other, "We should choose a leader and go back to Egypt."

– Numbers 14:1-4

Because of their unbelief and discontentment they wound up stuck in the wilderness and died in the desert. Only Joshua and Caleb—the two spies who returned with an encouraging report—made it to Canaan.

LIFE'S MERRY-GO-ROUND

As a child I loved to ride the merry-go-round. It was a thrilling experience until the day I mounted a real horse and was spoiled forever.

I constantly meet those who have bought into the merry-go-round philosophy of life, and they just keep spinning, going around in circles—from one bad relationship to the next, from one dead-end job to another. If they would only realize God has something far better than what they have settled for.

It's time to break the repetitive cycle and head for the land of promise.

LIGHT MY WAY!

Have you ever tried driving at night without your headlights? I wouldn't recommend it—unless you have a fondness for fender-benders!

In this dark, morally bankrupt world, without God you will eventually become blinded and crash.

In this dark, morally bankrupt world, without God you will eventually become blinded and crash.

Only the Lord can truly illuminate your path. Remember, He *built* the road and knows every mile-marker.

Trust in the Lord with all your heart

and lean not on your own understanding;
in all your ways acknowledge him, and
he will make your paths straight.

– Proverbs 3:5-6

Keep On Driving

I've seen a few episodes of the one-hour VH1 television specials called "Driven." They document the road to success of some of today's pop celebrities —people including Celine Dion and Shania Twain.

Every achiever will tell you, "It's impossible to go forward looking in your rearview mirror."

It's basically a program which details the long, hard grind from obscurity to fame.

I love the title of the show because it lets us know that if we want to rise above average we must be *driven*—motivated by the passion of our journey—never giving up regardless of what comes our way.

Every achiever will tell you, "It's impossible to go forward looking in your rearview mirror."

And Jesus said unto him, No man, having put his hand to the plow, and looking back, is fit for the kingdom of God.

– Luke 9:62

It's the plow which breaks up the ground and makes it possible for seed to be planted—it's the start of the eventual harvest.

God is always looking ahead. His decisions are made with eternity in view—and with His help I'm moving to higher ground.

GET IN THE GROOVE!

The most important lesson I learned during those years was to stay both consistent and persistent.

I learned in sports you'll have both good days and bad. There were times when I was "in the groove" and it seemed I could do no wrong. Then there were moments I'd rather forget about—I couldn't win for losing!

The most important lesson I learned during those years was to stay both *consistent* and *persistent.* With that approach you eventually find your rhythm of success.

Now that I am on a spiritual team, I appreciate consistency more than ever. If I stay steady—plowing ahead day after day, I find there is a certain momentum which carries me forward.

With childlike faith, I believed Jesus when He said "I am the way"—and I've been following Him ever since.

Opportunities don't fall off trees! When the Lord calls, drop everything you're doing and head His direction—to the place He leads. Stop complaining about your circumstances and start advancing.

Stay with what you know to be right.

THE GRAND MAZE

I remember the time we took our youth group to Panama City Florida. While there, we decided to check out the Grand Maze at Coconut Creek. It was billed as the largest maze ever constructed at that particular time.

The idea is to see who can go through the maze the fastest. They give you a time card to punch when you enter and when you finish.

"Easy," I thought, "This is going to be a breeze." Famous last words!

Once I entered the maze I realized just how it got it's name. It really was "grand." I was surrounded by walls eight feet high that seemed to go on forever. The entire labyrinth is the size of a football field!

Everywhere I turned was one more dead end. And just when I thought I was making progress, wham! Another wrong path. Again and again I was retracing my steps trying to find the exit.

Everywhere I turned was one more dead end.

I have to admit it—I was stumped. Some of the kids in our group made it to the check towers in the middle of the maze and were already having their card stamped. There I was, still wandering around. It was frustrating!

But just when I thought all hope was lost, some of the young people took pity on me and began yelling from the towers overhead, hollering out directions—"Go right! Turn left!"

After listening and following their cues, I was able to successfully find my way out.

Finally, I climbed the stairs of the tower and looked

down on the maze; the right path was so obvious. I could see every dead end and every route of escape.

It's amazing what a change of perspective will do.

A NEW VANTAGE POINT

When I was new in ministry, still in my teens, there were countless times I felt just as frustrated as being lost in that maze. On occasions, I thought no one respected me because of my age— or they felt I didn't *deserve* to be a youth pastor.

More than once I wanted to give up and just be a regular teenager. I was tired of hitting those dead ends and not being able to find my way out.

I sought God's help and He began to lift me up—higher and higher.

That's when I sought God's help and He began to lift me up—higher and higher. Before long I could see the larger picture as it zoomed into focus. Suddenly, from this new vantage point, the puzzle of life didn't seem so impossible.

The Lord expanded my vision and revealed His will. What a view!

Start Living "On Purpose"

As a result of reading this book, I pray you have a new perspective on what God has planned. We've talked about your dream, your drive and your destiny. In reality, however, it's not only about you!

Make a commitment to the Lord that you will not settle for anything less than *His* promise, *His* plan and *His* purpose for your future.

Oh, there's plenty you can accomplish on your own, yet what a lonely, hollow existence that becomes. It's so much better when you team up with the One who knows all about you—and loves you anyway. You see, He created you with something exceptional in mind. Are you ready to fulfill His plan?

Have a talk with your Father. Say, "Lord, You can count on me. I'm living my life on purpose!"

Notes

For a complete list of books
and tapes by the Author
or to schedule him for speaking
engagements, contact:

Alan Mushegan, Jr.
Gospel Harvester Church
Fusion Ministries
1521 Hurt Road
Marietta, GA 30008

Phone: 770-435-1152
Internet: www.iamfusion.com
Email: getfuzed@iamfusion.com